THE LIVING WORLD OF
DANCE

THE LIVING WORLD OF
DANCE

Artistry in Motion

Jack and Linda Vartoogian

with Carol Cooper Garey

a division of U.S. Media Holdings, Inc.
115 West 18th Street, New York, NY 10011

Endpapers: Sato Takako's Ryukyuan Dance Company, "Chibari Daiko."

Page 2 photograph: Young dancers at Pura Desa Temple, Singapadu, Bali, performing the Rejang.

Above: Vanaver Caravan dancers clogging.

Page 143 photograph: Peggy Lyman, "The Desperate Heart."

Page 144 photograph: Jeanne Solan/Nederlands Dance Theater 3, "So Sorry."

Photographers' Acknowledgements
From the time we first photographed Maurice Béjart's "Nijinsky: Clown de Dieu," in November 1972, we are fortunate to have been helped, encouraged and made welcome by hundreds of dancers, dance companies, choreographers, publicists, lighting and production managers, producers, picture editors, writers and dance fans whose numbers are too many to mention individually in this limited space. Our hope is that when those who have facilitated our tasks in cities and venues across America and around the world see this book, they will recognize that we are acknowledging them and will accept our deepest thanks.

Copyright © 1997, Saraband Inc.

All photographs copyright © Jack Vartoogian and © Linda Vartoogian

Design copyright © Ziga Design

This edition published in 1997 by SMITHMARK Publishers, a division of US Media Holdings, Inc., 115 West 18th Street, New York, NY 10011.

SMITHMARK books are available for bulk purchase for sales, promotion, and premium use. For details, write or call the manager of special sales, SMITHMARK, Publishers, 115 West 18th Street, New York, NY 10011.

Cataloging in Publication data available.

Produced by: Saraband Inc, PO Box 0032, Rowayton, CT 06853–0032.

ISBN: 0-7651-9920-3

Printed in China

10 9 8 7 6 5 4 3 2 1

EDITORS: Sara Hunt, Robin Langley Sommer
EDITORIAL ASSISTANT: Nicola J. Gillies

WE DEDICATE THIS VOLUME
TO OUR MOTHERS

Contents

Why Photograph Dance?

*"The dance is an art in space and time.
The object of the dancer is to obliterate that."*
— Merce Cunningham

The challenge could not be more obvious: within a static medium, how may one presume to convey the dynamic elements of an art form defined by movement?

Dance and song provide a particular seduction, in that each relies ultimately only upon those qualities with which the human body may seek unembellished expression. That is surely not to say that certain tools cannot enhance the telling—music, costumes, sets and choreography often do just that—but the principal agent remains the human body itself. These most portable of talents are carried *within* one's person; no tools—instruments, brushes, even cameras—are necessary for their execution.

Consequently, an observer must ponder carefully how best to evaluate and describe these deceptively simpler arts. For them there need be no paper upon which to place thoughts or score, no brush or canvas to give shape and color to one's expression, no instrument by which to express sounds passed from heart and brain to eye and ear. Dance is a naked art; adornments to which we may be accustomed are merely that.

From the most highly formal and choreographed to the most spontaneous and uncontrived, no dance is ever performed in precisely the same manner as it has been before, nor will it ever again repeat itself exactly. Highly academic techniques, extemporaneous expressions of movement, and all their varied offspring obey this cardinal rule.

So for us the answer is here: let us show the essence of *this* moment, of *these* performers in *these* moments. Let us take the journey backward and learn of the general by examining the particular, the unique. Let us show in moments of stillness the heart of what moves.
— Jack and Linda Vartoogian

Opposite: Lila York/ Paul Taylor Dance Company, "Esplanade."

Far Left: Elise Monte, George White, Jr./Martha Graham Dance Company, "Errand Into the Maze."

Left: Christine Dakin/Martha Graham Dance Company, "Snow on the Mesa."

Below: Suzanne Farrell, Sean Lavery, "Romeo and Juliet."

Introduction

*"When you do dance, I wish you a wave o' the sea,
that you might ever do nothing but that."*

—WILLIAM SHAKESPEARE, *The Winter's Tale*

Metaphorically described as poetry in motion, dance has inspired poets through the ages. Countless others, from all walks of life, have embraced the challenge of capturing in words this essentially non-verbal art. While essays, reviews, books, narratives and dancers' own testimony all help to preserve the myriad historic, intellectual and cultural meanings associated with the remarkably diverse world of motion, it is the living act of dancing that engages all our senses—whether as performers or audience. And since dance is a primal instinct and a compelling form of expression, what words could approach an adequate description of its texture?

The aim of this highly photographic album is to allow the very soul of dance to stimulate a personal response by involving the reader in movement as directly as possible. Through powerful images, we explore here aspects of the landscape of dancing as ritual, drama, social intercourse, celebration, self-expression, professional discipline and abstraction—sometimes even to the extreme of

Opposite: *Dudley Williams, Maxine Sherman/Alvin Ailey American Dance Theater, "Later that Day."*

Below: *Aubrey Lynch III Déjà Vu Dance Theatre, in rehearsal.*

absolute stillness. Cultural or sacred meanings are added to the visual impressions in concise descriptive form to convey context to the moment captured in each photograph.

While any form of dancing must be experienced firsthand to be appreciated fully, the magnificent abundance, beauty, impact, power and subtlety of the world of dance—the sheer multitude of possibilities inherent in the human body—can be comprehended only through a

collection that brings together many such contrasting moments. This lavish album is the result of the artistry, patience, technical mastery and decades-long commitment of Jack and Linda Vartoogian, whose curiosity has inspired them to travel the globe, and to keep apace with the constant stream of artists who visit their home city, New York.

Dancing is not neatly categorized. Discipline and precision are essential to many forms of dance, while spontaneity and improvisation characterize others. Introspection may be required of devotional and meditational dancers, yet others, including theatrical storytellers and courting couples, direct their focus outward to their audience or partner. Any broad divisions in this fluid range of possibilities are necessarily somewhat arbitrary. Accordingly, we have begun our exploration with a simple, visual gallery of arresting images in the opening chapter, Portfolio. Those for whom dance is a profession are featured in chapter 2, The Dancer's World. Traditional and ceremonial dances that form an integral part of the lifeways and cultural heritage of a particular society are shown in chapter 3, Dancing Around the World. In chapter 4, Let's Dance, the diversity of social dancing around the world is emphasized. While there is considerable overlap among these themes, we believe the chapters present a reasonably balanced picture of the many forms of dance—as living tradition, occupation, hobby or leisure activity.

Professional dance takes many forms, from traditions like ballet that are considered an art form, to those regarded simply as popular entertainment, like the chorus line. There are, however, commonalities in the lives of professional dancers in all of these fields. All require total commitment to punishing demands of long hours, physical endurance through repeated class and rehearsal; and restrictions in the personal life including, for many, weeks or months spent away from home on tour. Professional dancers are not simply gifted, or even created from years of dedication and practice—they must possess, in addition to these qualities, a drive or compulsion. Having chosen to enter a world where financial security and career longevity are virtually unknown, many dancers insist that they made no conscious choice: they dance because they desire it, because they were born to do it.

The live performance is of paramount importance to the professional dancer. The countless hours spent in rehearsal are geared toward "the real thing," an event that is greeted with fear, anticipation and excitement. However personally fulfilling the life of a dancer may be,

Below: Erik Bruhn, "The Moor's Pavane" rehearsal.

the success or failure of his or her career depends on the reaction of the audience and critics to each new performance. Whatever feelings of nervousness the dancer experiences before going on stage must be brought under control once the performance begins. Make-up, costume, stage lights and the presence of spectators combine to create an atmosphere entirely different from that of the rehearsal room. Some dancers find that

Below: *U Win Maung, Burmese dancer.*

their sense of self evaporates on stage; they feel transported to fully assume the identity of their role—and perhaps it is this very transcendence that can leave the audience breathless. In The Dancer's World, we profile some of the contemporary "greats" of professional dance, as well as glimpsing their world of individual training, rehearsal, costume and make-up.

The phenomenon of dancing is universal, transcending all national and cultural boundaries. People dance for all kinds of reasons, yet the vehicle for their expression is the same. In the "developed" world, dance is largely perceived as a profession or hobby. However, indigenous traditions survive around the globe wherever dancing is an element of daily life. Dances may perpetuate a tribal or cultural identity; celebrate heritage in the form of retelling a legend; worship a deity; call upon the gods for healing, help or good fortune; or express a political sentiment.

The latter category, dance as a political expression, is exemplified in many forms: often, dances become popular as statements of defiance and solidarity in the face of slavery, colonization and repression, examples of which are drawn here from the Caribbean, South Africa and Cambodia. Sacred and devotional dances abound on all continents. From Japan, Indonesia, India and the Americas, dance as worship is also illustrated on these pages. Folk dances that tell stories of a shared history or accompany traditional music are shown from Europe and Africa.

Often accompanied by elaborate costumes, face- and body-painting and ritualistic or symbolic props, these local dance traditions around the world share only two features: the universal instinct of body movement, and the preservation

of a cultural heritage through dances that are passed down generations.

In Let's Dance, we explore just a small selection of the ways in which people dance for leisure: as a social activity or simply for the sheer pleasure of dancing. Their individual movements may reflect the essence of joy experienced when the music calls to them, urging them to move, to sway, to leap, to dance. Rebellious youth find in dancing a means to define an identity. Couples court each other on the dance floor, sometimes by sharing a dance with highly stylized steps and movement, in other cases using erotic or seductive gestures. Dancing can be a tangible expression of what is often inexpressible otherwise. Young children spin and leap with unself-conscious exuberance. Teenagers find a sense of belonging by dancing with their peers. Friends dance together to share music and move-

ment that provide a feeling of enjoyment and release from daily pressures.

"O body swayed to music, O brightening glance,/How can we know the dancer from the dance?" asked W.B. Yeats, rhetorically ("Among School Children"). And in the fantasy world of Alice's wonderland, Alice is asked: "Will you, won't you, will you, won't you, will you join the dance?" The desire to lose oneself in dance is neither acquired nor taught; it is as natural as breathing. Whether our movements are improvised or learned, spontaneous or choreographed, performed alone, in groups or for an audience, each individual moment in movement is unique and has its place in the living world of dance. In tribute to this world, Jack and Linda Vartoogian have created a significant archive of stunning, vibrant images that combine to capture its essence.

Above: Mikhail Baryshnikov and potential hoofers from the National Dance Institute.

Above: Paul Taylor Dance Company, "Mercuric Tidings"

Previous pages: Rudolf Nureyev, "Apollo"
Maya Plisetskaya, "The Dying Swan"

Below: Nederlands Dans Theater, "Svadebka"

Following pages: Pilar Rioja, "Guajira"
Myung Soo Kim, "Jae Suk Chum"

Above: *Cloudgate Dance Theatre, "Nine Songs"*

Right: *Gelsey Kirkland/American Ballet Theatre, "Theme and Variations"*

Below: *Lowell Smith, Virginia Johnson/Dance Theatre of Harlem, "Greening"*

Above: *Mevlevi ("Whirling") Dervishes of Konya, Turkey*

Following pages: *Barton Mumaw, "Gnossienne"*
Richard Cragun, "Fetish"

Above: *Lane Sayles/José Limon Dance Company, "Psalms"*

Below: Merce Cunningham, "Summerspace" rehearsal

Opposite: Bando Tamasaburo, "Kanegamisaki"

Above: Sankai Juku, "Kinkan Shonen"

Below: Takako Asakawa/Martha Graham Dance Company,
"Primitive Mysteries"

Below: *Yuriko Kimura/Martha Graham Dance Company, "Primitive Mysteries"*
Above: *Naanim Timoyko, Nélida/Tango Argentino, "Milonguita"*

Left: *Vanessa Harwood/Universal Ballet Company, "Giselle"*

The Dancer's World

"The chosen few who have the magic are freighted with power and hope," wrote doyenne Agnes de Mille in her handbook for young dancers. She added that "the greatest stars have not always been beautiful, but all have had the royal prerogative of commanding with every tiny gesture total, rapt, heart-hungry attention." In the final analysis, the professional dancer conspires to transform a natural instinct into an art form.

Arthur Mitchell, founder of Dance Theatre of Harlem, believes that dancing is inborn: "Before a child is even out of the womb, it kicks—and kicking is dancing." But what propels dancers to undergo the demands of training for the professional arena? Rudolf Nureyev described it as a kind of possession. He claimed that he felt so alien on the stage that he was driven to perform. "Once on [the stage], I am lost," he said. "It's like a sacrifice—and I give of myself completely. The moment I'm on stage, things become multiplied and magnified. It's like having an atom reactor inside of me. There is a chain reaction and, suddenly, my whole body bursts into flames."

The roots of ballet, and Western theatrical dance in general, can be traced back to Italy's Renaissance, and we can find clues to these roots in the writings of a Jewish ballet master named Guglielmo Ebreo (William the Jew) of Pesaro, himself a pupil of the influential early dance theoretician, Domenico de Piacenza. Guglielmo emerged from humble beginnings to teach the royal children at Naples. His 1465 treatise "On the Practice of the Common Art of Dancing" probably served as a textbook for dance masters of his time. It furnished a list of requirements for a theatrical dancer, including memory, rhythm, a sense of space, grace, lightness, style, plasticity and mood. According to Walter Sorell, dance critic and historian, Guglielmo's contribution is "one of the earliest on which the huge pyramid of theatrical dancing rests."

Theatrical dance performances became an increasingly popular form of entertainment throughout Europe during the eighteenth century: when the Paris Opera Ballet School opened in 1713, dancers began to soar. By the nineteenth century, the ballerina had become an icon among patrons of the arts. The male dancer's role was to support and enhance her performance.

To the legendary Ruth St. Denis, dance was not so much a career as a mission. She believed that at its highest function, dance could enable one to grow beyond his usual limitations. With Ted Shawn, her partner and husband, she propelled this performing art into a new, expressionistic idiom. From their Denishawn School and company emerged many highly talented and accomplished artists, including the great Martha Graham.

Opposite: Isadora Duncan's "Valse Brilliante" as re-created by Salt Lake City's Repertory Dance Theatre.

Modern dance, which developed from the ballet tradition, harks back to primal movements as the real starting point for the professional dancer. Rather than choreographing dances to narrate a story, as in classical ballet, modern movements tend to express a more abstract, personal meaning or emotion. A parallel transition is seen in the emergence of Butoh from traditional Japanese ritual and theatrical forms.

The paths to professional ballet can be traced through the footnotes that only the artist can provide. Natalia Makarova, the most famous Russian ballerina of her day, began to study dance only accidentally, having gone with friends to the Palace of Pioneers in St. Petersburg intending to enroll in a gymnastics group. Had that particular mixup not taken place—at that particular time and in that particular place, eventually leading her to the Kirov School—she says she would have become a doctor, an architect or a linguist, following in more traditional family footsteps. For Robert

Right: George Balanchine's "Apollo" has challenged male dancers since its creation in 1928. Igor Zelensky, who performs today with both the Kirov and New York City ballets, displays textbook-perfect placement in dress rehearsal for a Kirov performance.

Left: *One of the most moving creations by controversial choreographer Maurice Béjart is "Songs of a Wayfarer," set to Gustav Mahler's poignant song cycle. It is performed here by Jorge Donn (front) and Daniel Lommel, both of whom were principals in Béjart's Ballet of the XXth Century.*

Joffrey, the passion to dance was triggered by Fred Astaire and Gene Kelly. Tap led him to a teacher whom he hoped would transform him into another Astaire; instead, his mentor steered him toward ballet. Months later Joffrey found himself on stage in "Petrouchka" with the famous Leonide Massine. "I remember Massine dancing so brilliantly, and he became my idol," said Joffrey, who aspired to have his own ballet company. Thus, "Petrouchka" played a part in the genesis of the Joffrey Ballet.

The professional dancer often feels responsible for teaching others, to perpetuate a tradition through the artist-to-artist contact that best keeps a living collective memory intact. Tina Ramirez followed in the footsteps of her teacher when she honored a promise to take over New York's Ballet Hispanico school. By reaching out beyond the studio to city schools, she offered young people opportunities to explore new possibilities through dance, as have other founders of prominent dance schools, including Arthur Mitchell and Eliot Feld. Since the Seventies, Ramirez has used her school to foster appreciation of Hispanic culture through classes and concerts. To date, she has reached more than 30,000 students across the United States.

Inspiration, talent and the example of great dancers may be crucial starting points, but these factors are only a beginning on the often grueling road to professional dance. Dedication is paramount: aside from the long working hours, the dancer is never off duty from the essential priority of maintaining his or her

Above: The island of Taiwan bursts with creative artistic energy, often supported by a government interested in showing its people's talents to the rest of the world. Here, choreographer Tao Fu-Lann and her company, Tao's Dance Theatre, perform a beautiful and mysterious piece entitled "The Vase" at the Taipei Theatre, in New York City's Rockefeller Center.

crucial "tool of the trade"—the body. From an early age, in common with other athletes, a dancer's need to remain in peak condition requires innumerable sacrifices, and any sense of job security is illusory. Concentration, discipline and stamina—both physical and mental—are essential. Every athlete's career is relatively brief, and "early" retirement, even from such a short career, can result at any time from injury.

For the dancer, the financial rewards achieved through performance and sponsorship are unlikely to be considerable even at the height of a career, and a personal life necessarily built around hours of class, rehearsal and performance—

sometimes involving long periods away from home—adds even greater demands to those faced by other athletes. Along with the extraordinary sacrifice, commitment and natural ability, luck, too, can play a part. Canadian artist Karen Kain had already achieved considerable success when Nureyev first met her, but his "discovery" of her remarkable talent provided a decisive boost to her career.

The demands of dancing for a living are, of course, common to "popular" entertainers as well as to their counterparts in dance forms more widely perceived as "art." Chorus line, tap and jazz dancers require a similarly grueling schedule of fitness, training and rehearsal.

Precision timing is just as crucial to the dancers in a popular musical as it is to ballet performers. On stage, the heat and glare of the lights, theatrical make-up and costumes—which may be cumbersome—impose additional burdens, which must be borne without apparent effort. From the Kirov Ballet through Riverdance and the Rockettes, each individual performer must remain vigilant in observing the rules of the dancer's world and must produce a fresh display for each new audience.

By its very nature, the life of a professional dancer reflects an urgency and single-mindedness foreign to the rest of us. Martha Graham condensed it to two brief sentences: "A dancer's instrument is his body bounded by birth and death. When he perishes his art perishes also."

Left: Modern dancer/choreographer Trisha Brown transformed one of her early solos into an intriguing pas de deux for herself and Mikhail Baryshnikov, entitled "You Can See Us." The piece, with music and costumes by the artist Robert Rauschenberg, was first performed in 1995.

Profile: Rudolf Nureyev

Nureyev! More than any other, this single name, three simple syllables, has meant "Dance" to the world in the last four decades of the twentieth century. When Rudolf Nureyev made his London debut in 1961, one commentator wrote, "It was as if a wild animal had been let loose in a drawing room." His exotic physicality and ability to entrance

audiences made him the icon of ballet, one who gave it a virile new body and who paved the way for two later defectors, Natalia Makarova and Mikhail Baryshnikov. On these pages, Nureyev is shown in class, performing the famous Nijinsky role in *"L'Après-midi d'un faun"* with the Joffrey Ballet, and partnering ballerina Monica Mason in the Royal Ballet production of *"La Bayadère."*

Profile: Natalia Makarova

Once in the West, Russian ballerina Natalia Makarova found many ways to display her virtuosity. Here we see her in arabesque as she rehearses "Don Quixote" with Alexander Godunov and (opposite, top left) demonstrating her extraordinary flexibility as she prepares for her role in "Le Rossignol" with teacher and coach David Howard. A flamboyant stage personality, Makarova dazzled audiences with the sexiness of her toe-to-the-top-hat turn in Roland Petit's "Blue Angel," and welcomed the opportunity to appear in a 1984 gala with New York's Radio City Rockettes, for which she is shown rehearsing (opposite, below).

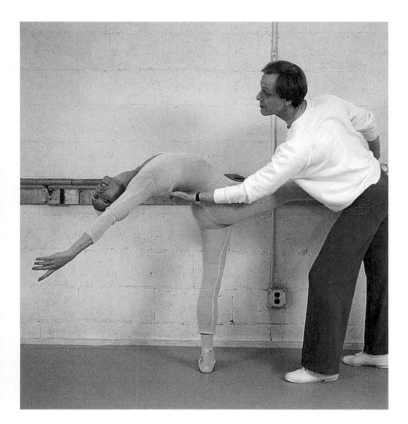

Profile: Mikhail Baryshnikov

Mikhail Baryshnikov's extraordinary range of physical accomplishments and purity of style surely qualify him as "an acrobat of God," Martha Graham's description of dancers with such consummate skill. A soloist with the Kirov Ballet at the age of eighteen, he quickened the pulse of American audiences during the late Seventies and Eighties, his era as premier male ballet dancer. Baryshnikov launches himself into space during Eliot Feld's "Santa Fe Saga" (opposite, above); in the other three images, all from his years at American Ballet Theatre, he performs "Swan Lake" with Makarova (right); his own version of "The Nutcracker" (left); and, with Marianna Tcherkassky (above, at left) and Martine van Hamel, demonstrates his remarkable affinity for more modern styles in Twyla Tharp's sassy "Push Comes to Shove."

Profile: Karen Kain

Without doubt Canada's most famous dancer, Karen Kain's beauty and style have brought her and the National Ballet of Canada international acclaim. In a partnership with Nureyev from the Seventies, she is shown as "Odile," the "Black Swan" in Act III of Tchaikovsky's "Swan Lake." Resplendent in white, above, she dances a solo from "Raymonda" as part of a touring company put together by Natalia Makarova in the early Eighties.

Profile: Jorge Donn

Jorge Donn was *the* Béjart dancer, epitome of all that the choreographer wanted to express, and in many ways his dance alter ego. A passionate and charismatic performer, Donn is shown here in Béjart's "Bolero," choreographed to the Ravel score as an erotic dance ritual (opposite), and in a more conventional *pas de deux*, "The Divine," with Marcia Haydée (star of the Stuttgart Ballet for many years, and later its artistic director).

Profile: Cynthia Gregory

For most of her career, Cynthia Gregory was acknowledged as America's finest "home-grown" ballerina. In recognition of twenty years dancing with the Company, in 1985, American Ballet Theatre (ABT) threw a spectacular gala for her, culminating in the traditional "confetti-throw," the surest sign of New York *balletomanes'* love and affection. Outdoors, in vibrant blue, she dances Ruth St. Denis' "Waltz" at the Jacob's Pillow Dance Festival in Massachusetts, while she and one of her favorite ABT partners, Ivan Nagy, exemplify the classical purity of *"La Bayadère's"* famed "White Act" (below).

Profile: Donna Wood

Following Judith Jamison as Alvin Ailey's lead dancer could not have been easy. But Donna Wood's striking beauty and fluid grace won over audiences immediately. In "Cry," Ailey's paean to "all black women everywhere—especially our mothers," Wood captures the fire and intensity of this modern dance classic. Below, in Ailey's masterpiece "Revelations," set to African-American spirituals and ring-shouts, she leads the company in its rousing finale, "Rocka' My Soul in the Bosom of Abraham." To prove that there is movement even in stillness, Wood elegantly upstages New York City's famous skyline.

Profile: Kazuo Ohno

Now in his nineties, Japan's Kazuo Ohno continues to astound audiences the world over. As a young man he saw a performance by "La Argentina," the famous Spanish Flamenco dancer, and thereupon decided to dedicate his life to dance. In the early Fifties he met Tatsumi Hijikata, one of the leaders of the postwar rejection of Western dance forms that came to be known as Butoh (often translated as "Dance of Utter Darkness"). Over the years Ohno has added Expressionist influences and his own quirky aesthetic to create altogether singular imagery. Most often appearing in female roles, Ohno is seen on the opposite page in his "Ka Cho Fu Getsu" ("Flowers-Birds-Wind-Moon"). At right, he performs "My Mother," while below he prepares for a performance of "Suiren" ("Water Lilies").

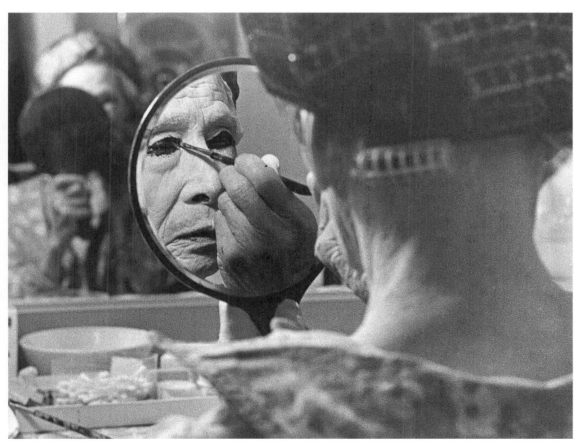

Butoh

Born in Japan during the 1960s, Butoh sprang from a spirit of revolt and a search for new means of expression. The Butoh dancer aims above all at baring his soul, at drawing us into an inner world, at exposing the most elemental humanity. While images employed are often ugly or grotesque, they are at other times hauntingly beautiful. Androgyny is often the vehicle for these journeys, in which the dancer's body is employed not as an exquisite object for aesthetic expression, but rather as a tool for exploration of the emotional landscape. Above, Sankai Juku, the most famous of modern-day Butoh groups and one which has influenced avant-garde dance around the world, presents "Jomon Sho"—a term that refers to Japan's early history. Poppo Shiraishi (above, right) brings pop sentiment to Butoh while the group Buto-Sha Tenkei (below, right) illuminates the stillness often at Butoh's core in "Nocturne."

More Than One Way to Tell a Story: Cinderella

While many ballet audiences seek the comfort of revisiting familiar stories, several contemporary choreographers have provided alternative ways of telling old tales. Pictured here are scenes from "Cinderella" as performed by the Kirov Ballet (left), the Fort Worth Ballet (below), Maguy Marin's Lyon Opera Ballet (opposite, top) and then-artistic director Rudolf Nureyev's version for The Paris Opera Ballet (opposite, below), in which Cinderella is a contemporary film star, surrounded by paparazzi.

Coppélia *(overleaf)*

"Coppélia," in its traditional interpretation by The Royal Danish Ballet, tells the tale of a dotty doctor who tries to breathe life into his workshop full of dolls. Maguy Marin again turns the tables by creating a roomful of "Coppélia" dolls, many of them men in drag, who force the young hero Franz to dance *for them*.

Les Sylphides *(page 61)*

"*Les Sylphides*," a plotless ballet also known as "Chopiniana" after its beautiful score, was choreographed by Michel Fokine in 1908. Dancers of Les Ballets Trocadero de Monte Carlo perform the dance *en travestie*. The all-male company regularly takes *pointe* class in order to properly undertake this traditionally female art. Below them, Mikhail Baryshnikov and dancers of American Ballet Theatre evoke the ethereal beauty of this timeless ballet.

Tap

Tap dancing's history is rooted in the clog dancing brought to America by Irish immigrants during the nineteenth century. One improvisation after the other added new rhythms to the form and new dancers to the forefront Contemporary tap dancing has been fueled by talents like four-year-old Zvi Wright, imitating his hero Maurice Hines, the seasoned star of "Sophisticated Ladies." Tap and jazz took a leap into the future when Savion Glover (opposite, below right) stomped onto the stage with a style he calls "hittin'," using a flat foot instead of the balls of the feet. Greg Hines shows his brand of expertise (near right), while dancers of L.A. Jazz Tap Ensemble (above) go through their paces in a more strictly theatrical setting.

Show-time Around the World

Tokyo's famed all-female Takarazuka Revue
Company (below) has been infusing traditional
Japanese drama with the lively spark of Western
musicals since 1914. It has staged full Broadway
productions in essentially original versions. After
enormous success in Paris, "Black and Blue"
(opposite, top) brought African-American jazz
and blues back home, to play for years on
Broadway. Radio City Music Hall's high-stepping
Rockettes (opposite, below) epitomize the ultimate
in precision and timing.

Expect the Unexpected
(*These and Following Pages*)

Sometimes your eyes sense something unusual, but your brain doesn't immediately tell you what it is! Young dancers emerge from beneath the skirts of Mother Goose in the Joffrey Ballet's production of "The Nutcracker," while below the camera does lie, in an unintentional double-exposure which makes an insightful comment on the Kirov Ballet's production of *"La Bayadère."* Opposite, another male *en pointe*, this time Ekathrina Sobechanskaya (*ne* Larry Ree, founder and director of the original Trockadero Gloxinia Ballet), performing "Panorama" in the largest tutu ever.

Following pages, 68: Choreographer Eliot Feld includes himself in "Doghead & Godcatchers," a sly commentary on dancing, choreographing and aging. On page 69, Rob Besserer assumes a decidedly undancelike position in Joachim Schlömer's "Beneath White Lilies," while dancers of Lyons, France's, Companie Azanie never leave their chairs during this long section of *A la vue d' un seul oeil.*

Leaps and Bounds

Boris Akimov as the happy-go-lucky "Mercutio" in
the Bolshoi Ballet's version of "Romeo and Juliet."
Karl Baumann of Momix (below) makes it look *so*
easy, as do Takako Asakawa in Martha Graham's
"Diversion of Angels" and Mikhail Baryshnikov in
Eliot Feld's "Variation on America."

Leaps and Bounds

Patrick Dupond (below) watches Sylvie Guillem toss off a *grand jeté* during a rehearsal of *"Le Corsaire"* with the Paris Opera Ballet. Not to be outdone, Natalia Makarova (bottom right) shows us her way in a rehearsal of the "Don Quixote" *pas de deux.*

Moses Pendleton (right), one of the most consistently inventive and idiosyncratic choreographers America has produced, re-creates his dance "Momix" in a room of his Victorian

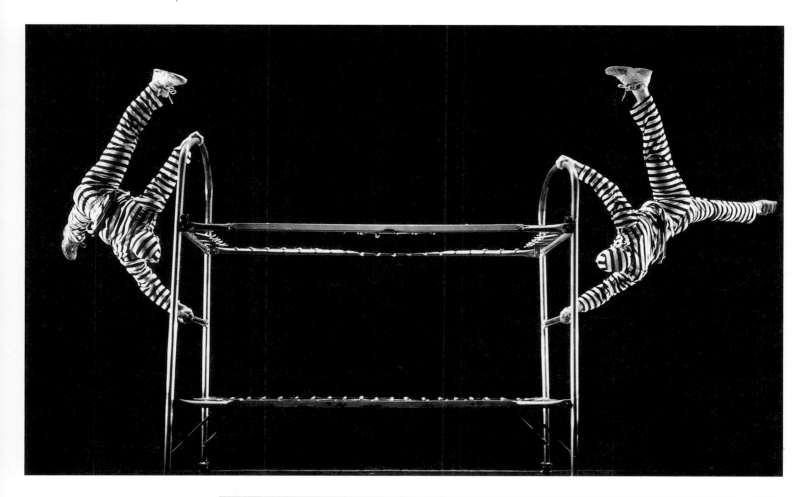

home; Erik Satie looks on. One of the founders of the now world-renowned Pilobolus Dance Company, Pendleton went on to name his next (and current) company "Momix," after this dance. Above, jail cells will never be the same: Momix dancers find still newer ways to surprise and delight audiences, as here in "Doing Time."

The Body as Sculpture

Dance is *always* about movement, even in its absence. One of its more interesting aspects can be learned at the crossroads of dance and photography, where photography can distill, illuminate and clarify one's vision by isolating forever a singular, fleeting moment. At those times, the human body takes on a variety of sculptural or abstract shapes that might otherwise pass unnoticed. In Murray Louis' "Moments," Rudolf Nureyev can be seen as reminiscent of Michelangelo's "David" or as the model for a textbook illustration of the ideal male body.

Below, dancers of Roland Petit's Ballet National de Marseilles in "Proust". Opposite, two quite different moments from Moses Pendleton's "Passion," to music by Peter Gabriel, performed by his Momix Dance Theatre.

Passing on the Tradition

Former New York City Ballet dancer Arthur Mitchell became determined to create a primarily black ballet company after the assassination of Dr. Martin Luther King. His Dance Theatre of Harlem has gone on to become a living symbol of King's— and Mitchell's—dream. Here, Frederic Franklin coaches young DTH dancers in "Swan Lake" with techniques and style he learned decades ago as a dancer, and later ballet master, with the Ballet Russe de Monte Carlo.

Young boys from the School of the Paris Opera Ballet demonstrate their technique. The Opera Ballet traces its origins to 1671, during the reign of Louis XIV. Thus, these students are the beneficiaries of over three hundred years of training and tradition.

Three young dancers concentrate on the intricacies of Flamenco at New York's Ballet Hispanico School, a training ground for young people who realize their potential through dance. Founded in 1970 by dancer Tina Ramirez, the school's aim is to promote an appreciation and understanding of the Hispanic world through traditional dances, along with ballet and modern dance techniques.

Passing on the Tradition

On page 78, children in Bali begin their instruction at an early age, aiming to attain the artistry already displayed by the young Indian dancer on page 79, top. The ultimate goal is to *perform*, as these Hispanic-American youngsters (below), an integral part of New York City's Los Peneros de la 21, already do. By participating in such activities they not only further their own artistic development, but also learn more about their greater cultural and religious traditions.

Whether at the Beijing Dance Academy, the Maryinsky Theatre in St. Petersburg, Russia, or elsewhere, ballet classes are conducted with strict rules which ensure that any trained dancer can comfortably take class anywhere in the world. Still, dancers can always find an individual way to relax, as does the Kirov's Larisa Lezhnina at far left. The ultimate accolade must finally go, however, to Rudolf Nureyev (right), who, even in class, never for a moment wavered in his ceaseless drive for perfection…and his consuming desire to inspire future generations by his own example.

Dancing Around the World

Dances that have evolved from the specifics of particular cultures form a rich tapestry in motion, each dance an expression of lifeways and beliefs from the earliest collective memories. Through traditional rituals, stories and costumes, indigenous dances may narrate the history, politics and religions of distinct cultures. To witness the customs expressed in movement is to become more familiar with worlds far outside one's own limited universe. While some traditions are nearly extinct, others survive, evolve and flourish. The fact that these traditions live on testifies to the allegiance of successive generations of dancers—whether every member of a village or tribe, or a handful of highly trained individuals—whose heritage is expressed through movement.

Dance as narrative is exemplified in the ancient Indian *Natya Sastra*, a sacred text that described specific movements for the head, eyes, nose, cheeks, lower lip, chin and neck, and sixty-seven hand gestures known as *mudras*. In all, 108 units of movement (*karanas*) were designated to enhance the physical expression of emotion.

The influence of Indian dance can be seen throughout South and Southeast Asia. As dance lore spread through the vast subcontinent, new forms were cultivated according to regional and social conditions. Indian dance today focuses on two leading schools, *Bharata Natya*

and *Kathakali*, both of which pay homage to the supreme god Shiva, classically represented as Nataraja, Lord of the Dance.

While *Bharata Natya* does involve storytelling or, at the very least, the conveying of messages and themes through movement, it is *Kathakali* and its near-cousin *Krishnattam* that represent Indian Dance-Drama supreme. Where *Krishnattam* concentrates on dramatizing particular episodes in the life of Krishna, *Kathakali* takes for itself the tales of the great Hindu epics of the *Mahabharata* and the *Ramayana*. Indians today still look to these epics, whether presented as ancient theatrical forms or in a television series, for guidance on the path of living a proper moral life.

A more vigorous style of dance emanated from western Bengal. Using the same epic sources, Chhau dancers leap and stamp in sensational masks and costumes. While a narrator sets the scene, drummers provide the rhythmic form for a dance that had been performed for centuries before it was revived and played to a wider audience in the 1960s.

The influence of *Natya Sastra* can also be found in Burmese dance, which is based on twenty-four single hand positions and twenty-eight eye movements. The most recent evolution of traditional Burmese dance expresses a range of emotion limited to expressions of joy or serenity, but the costumes are expressive in themselves, lavished with silver, gold and jewels.

Opposite: Evoking the glorious cherry blossoms of Kyoto, the Miyako-Odori *celebrates Spring and the Japanese love of nature's magnificent display, followed by the all-too-quick passing of its beauty.*

Storytelling in dance takes the form of recalling the history of a cultural group or enacting the legends of gods and spirits. Storytelling through symbolic gesture became highly refined in the Chinese opera, where several steps may indicate a journey and a few moments the passage of years. In the seventh and eighth centuries, Buddhist rituals and dance-dramas were exported from China and Korea to the Emperor's Court in Japan, where they were embraced and combined with surviving Shinto rituals in the form of *Gagaku*, to be performed at court functions and religious festivals. *Bugaku*, the dance component of *Gagaku* (meaning "beautiful or elegant music"), was originally performed in outdoor celebrations, but soon moved into the Palace and was rarely, if ever, seen outside the Imperial Household for a thousand years. *Kabuki*, in contrast to Imperial *Gagaku* and aristocratic *Noh*, is theatre for the masses, or at least for the then-emerging merchant class of early seventeenth-century Japan, which looked to it for loud, raucous, even risqué, entertainment. *Kabuki* was first developed and performed by women, whose sexual associations with patrons soon forced authorities to ban their participation in favor of young boys. This change, too, resulted in similar liaisons and further strictures, which ultimately resulted in the now-famous all-male performing tradition.

Both Bali's particular form of Hinduism and Javanese Islam have nurtured highly creative populations, for whom the arts permeate daily life. In both Java and Bali, not to mention the remainder of Indonesia's more than 13,000 islands, dance, as much a community activity as a skillful art, embraces the whole of drama. Its emotional range covers the romantic, heroic and farcical; in some forms in Bali especially, it is also religious rite. There, many of the dances relate to temple ceremonies. Entertaining the gods with food, dance, music and even a shadow play may be done simultaneously.

In the more restrained society of Java similar festivities occur, though in somewhat more subdued forms. There, the all-important quality is attainment of a moral and refined life. Again, throughout these societies, as throughout all of South and Southeast Asia, ancient Hindu epics coexist with similarly ancient local narratives to provide memorable moral lessons adhered to by millions of people.

In Cambodia, young, supple artists infuse dance with new energy as they learn from their elders, upholding a tradition born in the courts and temples of the Khmer rulers who built Angkor Wat. The legacy was nearly lost during Pol Pot's regime in the mid-1970s. Whole portions of court-dance repertoire perished with the dancers, teachers and musicians killed by the Khmer Rouge communist forces. Recovery of the national dance troupe's repertoire has

been attributed to one survivor, the late Chea Samy, whose recall of steps, gestures and stories has been vital in teaching young students a tradition equated with life itself. Thanks to her efforts and to those of organizations like the Cambodian Arts Project, among many others, dancers bring their beautiful serenity and equilibrium to a new generation of admirers. "Metamorphosed gazelles" is how poet Rainer Maria Rilke described the Cambodian dancers, whose hands reminded him of Buddha hands, for only they knew "how to sleep...to rest for centuries on laps."

In early Europe, as various tribal societies evolved along ethnic lines, primitive dance forms developed into characteristic folk or peasant dances. One example is England's Maypole dance, an offspring of older, Druidic tree-worshipping dances, in which the ribbons held by dancers who circle the pole symbolize the tree's branches. The Morris Dance of Lancashire originated in ancient weapon dances—a form of religious wor-

Opposite: On a steamy night in Singapudu, Bali, I Made Basuki Mahardika performs the baris, *a warrior dance in which the young dancer must, with stylized gestures and minimal expression, display the attributes of the soldier—from strength, ferocity and dignity to mercy and love.*

Below: Young Armenian-American women bring a centuries-old dance to Ellis Island, honoring those who entered America through its portals. With their graceful gestures and flowing costumes, they remind the onlooker of the nation's diversity and the freedom and security sought by generations of immigrants.

ship, not a war dance. Spanish folk dancing was much influenced by Andalusian folk forms such as Flamenco. Russia, Georgia and neighboring countries evolved vigorous, animated folk dances—perhaps the most famous being that of the Cossacks.

Africa south of the Sahara, usually considered an area highly conservative of tradition, especially dance, is, in fact, not particularly conservative at all, and traditional only in very specific ways. As in "traditional" societies the world over, culture—including dance—varies by region and ethnicity, and changes over time. New elements are introduced as older ones are discarded, in response to both internal and external forces. Dance-ceremonies usually take place at fixed dates on a ritual calendar, with the exception of such unpredictable events as deaths. But dance is only one element in most ceremonies, which are often aimed at placating nature or invoking its protection or blessing: music, storytelling and the ritual consumption of food and drink are included. Masked dances are common but not pervasive throughout the region; in them, the wearer is transformed from an everyday self into the identity of the spirit as defined by the society. Elaborate versions of masked dances are performed on the Guinea Coast, sometimes on high stilts requiring considerable agility. These ceremonies are not "shows" performed for an audience, or presented by one group for another in a Western sense. Rather, they are performed as an integral part of daily life, with the aim of reinforcing society's collective identity.

Tribal identity is also at the core of the dance traditions of aboriginal Australians, whose terrain gives rise to their steps. Men stamp their feet, digging into the earth as sand and dust swirls around them. Women, on the other hand, tread softly, leaving the high jumping steps to the men. Certain dances known as *djarada* are performed by women only when the men are away. Of all the rituals in which dance plays a crucial part, the initiation ceremony is the most sacred. On that occasion, youths become full members of their tribes, charged with the lifelong responsibility of honoring tribal identity.

No survey of indigenous dance, however brief, would be balanced without including native traditions of the Americas. Ritual and ceremonial dances have been performed by tribal groups throughout the Western Hemisphere for millennia, and some have endured to the present. The Cobéua Indians of Brazil still perform an age-old fertility dance wearing large artificial phalli. Other tribal dances of Central and South America centered on weapons, warfare, nature worship, hunting, crop rotation and initiation rites.

These categories were also represented in North America, where tribal legend as well as Western accounts testify to the significance of dance among various cultures from the Subarctic to the desert. Southeastern dance was depicted in watercolors by an explorer to North Carolina as early as 1585. So powerful was the ritual Sun Dance among the Plains Indians that it was considered a threat by the government. At nearly the same time, belief in salvation through sacred dance led the Paiute prophet Wovoka to form the Ghost Dance movement. Through days of praying, chanting and dancing in open-air circles, followers believed that the land would return to its former inhabitants and the white invaders would disappear. The movement led to a rebellion which ended in violence and the death of thou-

sands of Native Americans. So repressive were the U.S. government's subsequent restrictions that ceremonial dances were not allowed to resume until well into this century.

In the Subarctic and Arctic circles, the predominant emphasis in traditional dance is its integral role in shamanic rites. A hypnotic drumbeat, ritual mask or rattle, and communion with deities or ancestral spirits are all essential elements. A reverence for nature, even in such harsh environments, is perhaps even more evident here then elsewhere.

In extant tribal societies like those of Arizona's Hopi, dance still serves as a form of worship, with specific forms for different ceremonies. Today, many ceremonial dances can be experienced on Native ground, or at public presentations by such groups as the American Indian Dance Theatre. Others are never performed before outsiders. But in witnessing performances of the spectacularly costumed Eagle Dance or the complex Hoop Dance, one is privileged to glimpse momentarily the essence of a culture.

Above: In the rapidly setting sun of central Java, Sardono W. Kusumu improvises on classical Javanese dance movements at Plaosan Temple.

Opposite, above: The eternal struggle between good and evil literally takes center stage in this Kathakali dramatization of an episode in the renowned Hindu epic, the Mahabharata.

Opposite, below: The Formosa Aboriginal Dance Troupe includes young representatives of a number of different tribes indigenous to the island (now Taiwan), who strive to preserve their culture and ethnicity.

Varieties of West African Dance

Les Ballets Africains from Guinea (below) and
Senegal's National Dance Company (opposite, above)
combine both traditional and newer popular dance
styles and stories with Western ideas of choreography
and stagecraft to produce vibrant, didactic theatre
that is accessible to audiences everywhere. The
dances of the Ga people of Ghana are presented by
Odadaa! (opposite, below), a dynamic group led by
master drummer Yacub Addy. Dancers respond to
the percussive command of the drums, but at times
the lead drummers must react quickly to accompany
the dancers' rapidly improvised steps.

Congo Pygmies

At left, the Batwa and Ekonde peoples of the northern Congo present a dance evoking war and pleading for the protection of nature. Below, the Pende of the northwestern Congo are particularly renowned for their ritual masks, which are the link between spirits and mankind. Their songs and dances may praise Pende traditions, appeal to spirits, pass along humorous tales or lament parting.

Solidarity

The South African Zulu group Ladysmith Black Mambazo was founded in the 1960s by Joseph Shabalala. The *a capella* ensemble, which presents modern interpretations of traditional Zulu music and dance—incorporating both a strong anti-apartheid message and heartfelt Christian beliefs—received sudden international attention through their collaboration with Paul Simon. In 1991 Headman Shabalala, one of Joseph's brothers, was killed by an off-duty policeman; Ladysmith's message was only reinforced by this tragedy.

The Gumboot Dance was born in the mines of South Africa. Based on the percussive sounds of the slapping and stomping of boots, it is a powerful symbolic protest against the working conditions experienced by vast numbers of miners, a message underlined by the passionate slogans that sometimes accompany the dance. It is performed here by the Zimbabwean group Black Umfolosi, well known both as traditional performers and social activists.

Sensuality and Spirituality

Islam, perhaps more than some religions, defines much of what its adherents may do. But within such strictures, there has always been considerable flexibility. Belly dancing, as it is known in the West, grew out of the Muslim recognition, even appreciation, of human sexuality, allowing a woman to express her role as wife and mother...or her potential for those roles. While a young woman may perform similar dances at weddings, for example, she must still bow to a variety of cultural restrictions, which tend to keep her "protected" from men by the males of her family.

The Mevlevi Order of Dervishes (above), known throughout the world as the Whirling Dervishes, from Konya, Turkey, spin to induce spiritual ecstasy and trance, which will bring them complete communion with God. The Gnawi of Morocco (right), of mixed Sudanese, Berber and Arab ancestry, are both entertainers and spiritual intermediaries whose long ceremonies involve placating evil spirits, usually for healing purposes.

The Fiery Flamenco

Flamenco emerged from the gradual assimilation of the folk culture of the Spanish Romany (or Gypsy) people, who first settled in Catalonia in the fifteenth-century, with the ancient, predominantly Moorish Andalusian musical tradition, eventually to become Spain's national dance. It is an expression in music and movement of pride, poverty and tragedy. Its emotional intensity feeds on improvisation—the staccato steps of the dancer, the passion of a singer, the driving force of a guitar. Dancers talk of the *duende,* a spirit that enters them when they near exhaustion: this spirit is said to take control of the body, moving it in ways that are unique to each individual performance. Feet perform elaborate heel beats, from whispering to riotous. Hands clap in *palamadas,* defining the rhythm. Dresses swirl and arms carve elegant shapes in the air.

Lilliana Morales (left) and Martin Santangelo (opposite, right) typify the passion and commitment of the Flamenco dancer; (opposite, left), tradition merges with classical technique in the movements of a dancer in the National Ballet of Spain.

From Europe's Heartland

Diverse as the many villages from which they spring, Slovak dances portray the true folk character of their heritage. Through music, dance and traditional peasant costumes, the essence of each particular region is captured in a rich variety of styles from a broad selection of cultures. "Lucnica," the Bratislava-based song and dance ensemble (left), is composed of ballet-trained dancers, whose virtuosity enhances and theatricalizes folk patterns and steps, while remaining faithful to their original meanings.

Georgian Grace

Women of the Georgian State Dance Company glide through the *Narnari*, in an attitude of formal grace. Georgian women never dance on pointe, leaving "toe dancing" to the men, nor do the sexes ever touch in traditional dances. Situated on the Eurasian land bridge, Georgian culture reflects influences from the wide variety of peoples who have passed through the area for over two thousand years.

Russian Steppes

The diverse forms of Russian folk dancing are exemplified by the acrobatic and exuberant Moiseyev Dance Company. Since 1937 Moiseyev's dancers have popularized the folk dances—and through them the cultures—of the former Soviet Union. More importantly, numerous similar ensembles continue to appear, not only throughout these regions, but also in many other countries around the world, where vigorous interest in indigenous folk dance has often developed after a visit by this ensemble. Below, Company members perform "Polyanka," which reflects the dance's spirited Slavic origins.

Boys from Brazil

Second in popularity only to soccer, *capoeira* is Brazil's fast, graceful martial art dance. African slaves from Angola developed this form of martial art both to protect themselves and to fight for their freedom, disguising it as dance in order to practice it openly.

Viva Mexico!

Ballet Folklorico de Mexico celebrates the national spirit with vibrant costumes (opposite), colorful character dances and authentic music representing the diversity of the provinces. A seductive pairing of skirts and sombreros (below) contributes to the allure of this renowned company.

Carnaval da Bahia

In a kaleidoscopic frenzy of color, movement and sound, the dancers and musicians of the Balé Folclórico da Bahia (opposite) explode in a Samba Reggae, one of the newer popular dances to spring forth from this most African of Brazil's states.

Tales from Cuba

Los Muñequitos de Matanzas, Cuba's foremost practitioners of Rumba and Afro-Cuban religious music, have been entertaining at fiestas and *barrio* dances, and later in theatres and music festivals around the world, for forty-five years. At left, an *ireme*, or *diablito*, makes his appearance in the *Abakua* ritual, originally part of a men's secret society of Western Nigeria. Below, the *Guaguancó*, a contemporary Rumba of urban origin. A dance of pursuit, the man chases the woman and tries to possess her using various erotic gestures, while the woman tries to avoid him, turning away but looking back at him with flirtatious glances.

Native America's Diversity

Clockwise from above, these pages show: magnificently feathered members of the American Indian Dance Theatre performing the Pueblo Eagle Dance; a sacred, shamanic Inuit form based on the traditions of the Yup'iks from the Bering Sea coastal region; Hawaii's Polynesian-rooted Hula; Plains footwork, beadwork and quillwork during a women's "Jingle Dance" performance; and Kevin Locke performing the Plains Sioux Hoop Dance.

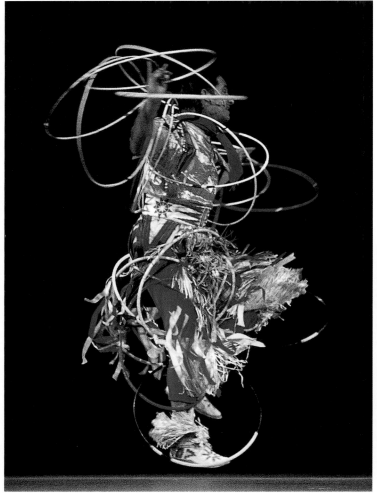

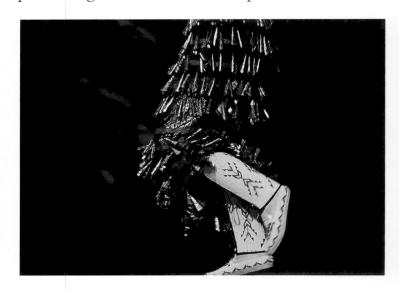

Chhau Dancers

From eastern India, Chhau originated as a martial drill with sword and shield, which evolved gradually as a distinctive dance form connected with the worship of the Hindu god Shiva (who is also known as Lord of the Dance). The unusual stances—often one-legged—and sudden leaps demand highly developed poise and strength. Here, in "Radha Krishna," Lord Krishna dances with his consort Radha, oblivious to the world around them (opposite).

Devotional Dances of India

Mallika Sarabhai, left, performs a devotion to Devi, Mother of the Universe, in the traditional South Indian dance style called *Kuchipudi*. As so many of Indian performing arts traditions, stories from the *Ramayana* and the *Mahabharata* are created in dance, song and music. Above, the legendary Guru Kelucharan Mohapatra celebrates his 70th birthday by dancing in *Odissi*, one of the seven principal classical Indian dance forms. This style, characterized by fluid movements and stunning sculptural poses, developed in the temples of the eastern Indian state of Orissa.

Colors of Korea

A rainbow of colors—primary and pastel—are reflected in this diverse selection of traditional movement and costume. Clockwise from left: "Pa'lmokjung Ch'um," an example of masked dance-drama showing one of eight monks who forsake their mountain temple and asceticism to flamboyantly sing and dance their way through the world; the National Dance Company of Korea performs a Fan Dance; Korean Living National Treasure Kim So Hee in an improvised folk dance greeting the harvest; "Kainjonmokdan," an elegant court dance dating from the early nineteenth century, wherein beautiful young women dance around a large vase filled with peonies, the traditional symbol of wealth.

Hypnotic Drumbeat

At left, the traditional Tsaatam Bii (Tsaatam Tribal Dance) recalls an ancestral custom: when men of the tribe returned from the hunt, their wives greeted them by dancing around the fire. The drum rhythms incorporated in this performance by dancers of the Mongolian People's Republic are an integral part of the dance.

Theatrical Gesture

One of Thailand's oldest forms of dance-drama, *Lakon Chatri* was developed by itinerant groups of performing artists who wandered the countryside playing to rural village audiences. Southern vernacular styles were mixed with the central Thai *lakhon* style to produce this genre, which is based on traditional Buddhist tales but frequently adds comic, often quite risqué, elements. Here, Anucha Tang-on, of the Pathumsilp Troupe from Petchaburi, portrays the hero Phra Apaimani.

Siberian-Asian Dance-Drama

Elza Levkovskaya of the Kamchadal people of north-eastern Siberia sings and dances the story of "The Wedding of the Birds," which comments on the improbability of different species living together. Dances like these, accompanied by singing cries imitating the sounds of the region's abundant wildlife, impart strong moral messages.

Folk Opera of Tibet

Both ancient legends and historic events of Tibetan culture are elaborately staged in the form of operas, operettas and dance dramas. Here, the Lhamo Folk Opera perform "The Story of Sugkyi Nyima," the tale of an ancestor king who was inspired to spread Buddhism through the land. The set design includes a depiction of the exiled Dalai Lama's imposing former residence, the *Potala*, in Lhasa.

A Lifetime to Learn

Cambodia's traditional court dance—unique and breathtaking in detail of gestures, from fingertip to eye focus, and glorious, rich costume—takes a lifetime to learn. But in the tragedy of the 1970s, these traditions were virtually exterminated, preserved only in secret, or by those fortunate enough to have escaped the brutality of the Khmer Rouge regime. At right, Malene Sam is rehearsing "Makhala," a dance to induce rain. Thirteen years earlier, a much younger Malene was already striving to attain the level of mastery of her mother, Chan Moly Sam (opposite, right). Like Sam Oeun Tes with her (left, with towering headpiece), Chan Moly Sam's understanding of dance will continue to develop. Below, Amarin Sam (Malene's brother) begins his dance journey as "Hanuman," the white monkey-general hero of the "Reamker," the Khmer version of India's *Ramayana*.

Tailoring to the Body

A venerable matron of the multifaceted art of Cambodian court dance, Kong Ros guides the traditional tailoring of the costume to Sam Oeun Tes's body. The patient dancer must stand still for many hours while the glittering, rich fabrics are painstakingly sewn into place, then again when the costume is removed after performance, as at left.

Beauty in Her Hands

Kong Ros tutors young dancers from the Cambodian Arts Project in the precision of body placement and subtleties of the signature hand gestures, which require seemingly endless stages of refinement to approach perfect beauty, as shown in this dancer's hands, below.

The Masks of Topeng Cirebon

In the sweltering heat of Plumbon village near the Indonesian city of Cirebon on the northern coast of Java, Arja Sujana, a master of the masked dance style known as *Topeng* dons the mask of the *Panji* cycle. With each metamorphosis, he says, the mask tells him what to do—and become: the ideal, refined, white-faced "Panji," who represents the highest ethical and social values of the Javanese; the androgynous "Rumiang"; and finally the angry, uncontrolled, red-faced "Klana" (or "Klono"), the embarrassing antithesis of "Panji," who suggests the dangers of an unexamined, irresponsible life. After proceeding through these and other masks of the cycle, the exhausted artist begins the slow return to his natural self.

From the Indonesian Archipelago

At left, nine beautiful Javanese dancers glide through "Bedhaya," the most sublime attainment of the courtly arts of Yogyakarta, the artistic and cultural center of Java. Their restrained emotions again reinforce the Javanese model of the ideal self. Right, a Sundanese dancer's scarves mirror the movements of his courtly counterparts. Below, left and right: Bali, Hindu Island of Mystery, where, in the village of Batuan, a masked dancer performs another style of *Topeng* at the local *banjar*, the term used equally for an open-air, communal building and those member-families who gather there. At a temple in Singapadu village, young girls, their hands gracefully recalling positions from Hindu *mudras*, welcome the gods in an ancient and formal procession known as *rejang*.

Classical Chinese Dance

Zhongmei Li, opposite, performs the "Peacock Dance," which combines Chinese classicism with influences from ethnic minorities—exotic as well to the Chinese. At right, a graceful dancer poised on a lotus-petal platform; below, the traditional Red Silk Dance, a gift to the U.S. of 1970s "ping-pong" diplomacy. This dance, part of the first post-war cultural exchange program between the countries, was performed at New York's Metropolitan Opera House in 1978.

Japan: From Theatre to Court

A small sampling from the extravagant profusion of Japanese dance forms. Clockwise from right: Bugaku, a thousand-year-old court dance as performed at Iwashimizu-Hachimangu shrine near Kyoto; the "Father and Son Lion Dance," *Renjishi*, from the Kabuki tradition; Yotsutake (also known as *Odori Kawadesa*), a colorful Okinawan dance performed on festive occasions, featuring brilliant headdresses which have become a virtual symbol of Okinawa; *Ai No Katami* or "Mementos of Love," a traditional dance style at once influenced by court dances and an important influence in itself on Kabuki.

Let's Dance

If, as Moliére said, the destiny of nations depends on the art of dancing, let's hope that every dance is a step toward a more joyful world. Certainly the world became a better place with the advent of social dancing, a metaphor for earthly pleasures. From the genteel court dances of the Renaissance to the steamy Tango of modern times, social dancing has played passionate roles in courtship and all kinds of communal activities. Virtually every society has its version of social dancing, an animated expression of the culture. The Waltz, for example, reflects the elegant energy of nineteenth-century Europe through the captivating music of Johann Strauss, father and son. "Touch dancing" evolved as couples whirled around the dance floor enjoying their intimacy in public.

While Europeans waltzed, Americans two-stepped, prompted by the march rhythms of John Philip Sousa. Meanwhile, Ragtime, born in New Orleans, set off a craze for athletic dances with names like the Turkey Trot and Bunny Hug. Couples were progressively closing in on each other—after four centuries of keeping their distance.

After World War I, social dancing took on the spirited attitude of the Twenties in America, epitomized by the Charleston. When Prohibition drove those thirsty for stimulation to Havana, Cuba, the Rumba was adopted by a new audience intoxicated by the Latin beat, and a cultural exchange was born. Equally intoxicating was the Tango, an Argentinean export that took Paris by storm. Tango fever finally hit North America and even Finland, where the dance remains a vital part of the culture today. The surge in Tango's popularity coincides with the interest in fitness, as ballroom dancing is embraced for its benefits to body, mind and spirit.

Historically, dance has helped to lift the spirits in woeful times. For example, the 1929 U.S. stock market crash motivated Hollywood to boost the nation's morale. Thus the musical extravaganza,

Opposite: Something in the balmy air of a New York City Central Park SummerStage concert invites a solo of free-spirited exuberance.

Left: The bandleader always gets the girl. Tito Puente does an impromptu cha-cha with singer/dancer Nydia Ocasio during the finale of a Latin Jazz concert in New York City's Harlem.

exemplified by Ginger Rogers and Fred Astaire, who inspired a generation of ballroom imitators. Eventually, after another world war, there was a new version of the hop: the Jitterbug or Boogie woogie, a nervous dance symbolic of the times.

Latin fever marked the Fifties in Europe and America, with Mambo, Cha-cha and Merengue on the rise. As Rock-and-roll records hit the airwaves, teenagers followed the beat with yet another kind of dancing—more gyration, less contact. By the Sixties, dance floors had become arenas for a dynamic

Chubby Checker creation: "Let's Do the Twist!" sent hips swiveling and arms pumping, as New York's Peppermint Lounge turned into a social mecca. The raging popularity of the Twist created spinoffs with names like the Monkey, Frug and Jerk. And the heat generated by these frenetic movements called for a new environment to house the mania. Paris responded with the disco—the nightclub that became a prototype for the world. Typically, the disco pulsated with recorded music blaring in cavelike settings where dancers went wild under

Above: Contemporary ballroom dancers exhibit their fluid skills with the same flourish as waltzing partners of another era.

Opposite: Sometimes violent, always frenetic, Slam Dancing at once demonstrated youth dissatisfaction and the need for community. From here, it was only a short leap (so to speak) to the Mosh Pit.

Above: *Musicians take to the streets in a celebration of pure joy. Two kids respond with Zydeco, born in southwest Louisiana as a gumbo of African-American, Caribbean and European cultures.*

the Woodstock Festival of 1969 and the British Punk explosion of 1977. Nameless dances produced by assorted acts of rebellion emerged around the world, from Amsterdam to Japan, where Rockabilly became a new ritual.

With the opening of New York's Studio 54 in the late Seventies, free spirits found a new venue for "anything goes" dancing. The urban Nineties version caters to a crowd that prefers a quieter, more intimate club setting with plush sofas for lounging near the dance floor.

While the social dancing of fashionable urban centers in the West has followed rapidly changing trends, most cultures enjoy indigenous social dance traditions that evolve more slowly, or are simply passed from one generation to the next. These may take the form of rite-of-passage or holiday celebrations, courtship rituals, political or historical expressions, or direct responses to the sounds and rhythms of a specific musical heritage. In South America and many Caribbean islands, for example, free-form movements translate into street carnivals. In Ireland and Scotland, ancient jigs and reels inspire extemporaneous dance, as at the traditional Gaelic all-night *ceilidh*, or simply an evening spent at the pub. All over Africa, people rocked to the beat of *Soukous*, a hard-driving musical style built upon Rumba rhythms that were imported from Cuba. This represented a turnaround—"You *can* go home again!"—since Rumba itself is rooted in the music brought to the New World by African slaves.

During the later part of the twentieth century, popular ethnic dance forms have found wider audiences and new participants. The club is only one of the options available to those determined to dance. For everyone who sets foot inside a club, there are dozens more

flashing strobe lights. George Bernard Shaw must have foreseen this craze when he referred to dancing as "a perpendicular expression of a horizontal desire."

In the disco, convention was abandoned for open expressions of sexual preference, racial equality and political unrest. What happened to the Western dance scene was a major display of liberation, as in

dancing to their own tune elsewhere. In China, for example, many residents of Beijing now start their days ballroom dancing in the park before they go off to work. In Connecticut, the School of the Hartford Ballet sponsors Dancing with Disabilities, whose participants explore space beyond the wheelchair. In New York, a downtown church hosts weekly English country dances evocative of Jane Austen's nineteenth-century novels. Dance dissolves boundaries and creates an unparalleled opportunity for self-expression.

From ancient times, dance has conditioned the body, relaxed the mind and freed the spirit. Born of spontaneity, dance needs no professional credentials to authenticate it. The universality of the dancing spirit shows itself in the street fair, the summer festival, the country hoedown, the disco, the community hall. All the world is, in fact, a stage for dance.

Above and left: Dancing feet of different cultures: barefoot glee at an outdoor summer festival in the American South; Step Dancing in the Irish tradition, which requires considerable stamina to keep up with the accompanying reels, jigs and hornpipes.

It Takes Two

To Argentineans the Tango is as much an obsession as a dance. Its roots can be traced to a Cuban slave dance. Tangomania, sparked in the bistros and bordellos of Buenos Aires, spread to the fashionable salons of Paris before it gripped the United States. In the 1930s, legendary singer Carlos Gardel fueled the obsession with rich baritone recordings of loneliness, unrequited love and death. Equally captivating was silent-screen idol Rudolph Valentino, whose dancing evoked male dominance, passionate love and seduction. With scarcely a powerful emotion left untapped, Tango endures as an addictive dance for all ages and levels of ability. As a vibrant example, dancers from "Tango x 2" recapture the moody sensuality of this legendary dance.

A Rite of Summer

The plaza of Manhattan's Lincoln Center becomes a stage at the annual July frolic known as Midsummer Night Swing, which attracts throngs of dance devotees. For a nominal fee, couples dance to live music against a backdrop of luminous buildings dedicated to the living arts.

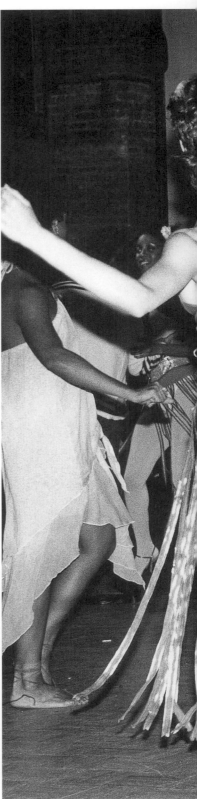

Disco Fever

In an atmosphere of total freedom at New York City's Studio 54, dancers sensationalize every primal move. The costumes follow suit—the only dress code is outrageous. A decade earlier, during the Sixties, European discos had set the stage for a universal boom in dance clubs as platforms for rebellion.

Stepping Out

Country Western is a state of mind, its two-stepping routines a tribute to dual coordination. The dress code, however casual, is inspired by cowboy regalia. Authentically American, Line Dancing took hold in the Sixties and has spread its charisma to all age groups and cultures. Here, in New York's Denim & Diamonds, Line Dancing is a nightly exercise in stepping and whirling to the Tush Push, Boot Scoot and Watermelon Crawl.

Break Dancing

In the late Seventies, city youth muscled into a macho dance form that emerged from the Black ghettos. Expressing "attitude," Break Dancing was a statement of pride as well as an irrepressible display of vitality, sophisticated choreography and acrobatic moves that amazed passersby and attracted admiring audiences.

Carnival!

In southwestern Louisiana, Mardi Gras (or Fat Tuesday) retains a close link to centuries'-old traditions from Europe. Costumes, masks and old French songs all propel participants toward the Midnight Hour, when reveling ceases and celebrants turn into worshippers for the forty-day observation of Lent. Similar celebrations typify other cultures as well. Below, a traditional Carnival-style samba line mixes New York theatre-goers and Brazilian dancers during a performance of a Broadway spectacle called "Oba-Oba '93."

Grooving on Stage

Soukous star Aurlus Mabele from the recently renamed Congo dances to the beat of his own band, Loketo, which means "Swing Your Hips" in Lingala, one of the Congo's major languages.

Below, expatriate Guineans from the audience join members of the Mamady Keita Drum Ensemble on stage, responding to their irresistible rhythms.

Nouveau Zydeco

Developing from the still-flourishing, but older,
Creole dance styles, Nouveau Zydeco dancers
emphasize even closer proximity and greater
angularity in their movements. The dancing and
music attract thousands every Labor Day Weekend
for the Original Southwest Louisiana Zydeco Music
Festival, held in a large field near Plaisance.

Rockabilly, Tokyo Style

A typical street scene in Tokyo's Yoyogi Park, where Japanese youth created their own pop culture with a distinctly American flavor. The result of mingling Black and Country music (not to mention Elvis Presley!), Rockabilly dance styles emerged in the Fifties. By the Eighties, Rockabilly was causing Japanese parents to look at their children with the same mixture of awe and confusion that Americans had felt in the previous generation.

Index